EYES ON
DOGS

Maggie Fischer

Silver Dolphin

Silver Dolphin Books
An imprint of Printers Row Publishing Group
A division of Readerlink Distribution Services, LLC
10350 Barnes Canyon Road, Suite 100, San Diego, CA 92121
www.silverdolphinbooks.com

Printers Row Publishing Group is a division of Readerlink Distribution Services, LLC.
Silver Dolphin Books is a registered trademark of Readerlink Distribution Services, LLC.

All notations of errors or omissions should be addressed to Silver Dolphin Books, Editorial Department, at the above address.

Written by Maggie Fischer
Designed by Haydee Yanez
Image Credits: Getty Images

ISBN: 978-1-68412-314-8

Manufactured, printed, and assembled Heshan, China. First printing, May 2018. HH/05/18.
22 21 20 19 18   1 2 3 4 5

CONTENTS

MAN'S BEST FRIEND

Originally bred for a multitude of tasks such as hunting, herding, or protecting, dogs have lived with humans for thousands of years. Dogs were the first animals to be domesticated. Affectionate, loyal, smart, and useful, dogs are popular pets for a good reason!

All over the world there are dogs that vary in size, shape, color, and even personality. They can be as tiny as six inches tall or weigh a colossal two hundred pounds! Some dogs have short fur, some have long locks—it all depends on the breed! A breed is a way of grouping dogs who have similar physical and behavioral traits.

good boy

Sit

So how do you decide which breed of dog is the right pet for you? Do you want a dog that can train for marathons with you or one to keep you company on the couch? Do you want to sink your fingers into thick, fluffy fur, or do you prefer the quick cleanup that comes with shorter coats?

Whether you're ready to pick a pet or just curious about cool canines, this book gives you a chance to explore different breeds and their sizes, appearances, personalities, and litter sizes (the number of puppies they can have).

So put your paws on the page and get ready to explore the wonderful world of dogs!

BOSSY AUSSIE

The Australian shepherd breed was developed in the United States of America, but was given its name because of its association with the Basque sheepherders who came to the United States from Australia in the 1800s. Incredibly intelligent and active, Australian shepherds are great working dogs, especially when it comes to herding. Although their natural instincts as guardians make them skilled farm dogs, Aussies have also worked as search and rescue dogs, seeing-eye dogs, and assistance dogs for the handicapped.

Australian shepherds are quick learners and extremely loyal, and they love to play! They make great family pets, but require a lot of exercise and activities that keep them challenged and busy. Their protective instincts are strong, and they thrive when they have a job to do. These bossy Aussies will keep you on your paws!

DOGGIE DATA

Country of Origin:
The United States of America

Average Lifespan:
13-15 years

Average Litter Size:
5-10 puppies

Average Weight:
30-50 pounds

Average Height:
18-23 inches

Coat Colors:
Black, red, blue merle and red merle

Did You Know?

As a breed, Australian shepherds are more prone than other dogs to having heterochromia, a condition in which they are born with two different-colored eyes. Sometimes, just a part of their eyes have a different color!

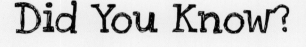

I'M ALL EARS

Basset hounds were first bred as hunting dogs in sixteenth-century France. With their low-set bodies, sturdy build, and keen sense of smell, they were perfect for following on horseback as they led the way to rabbits and other small game. In addition to their bulky bodies, basset hounds are characterized by their long, floppy ears, which help them track game by stirring up scents on the ground.

The basset hound makes a great companion and loves to snooze on laps so much that you may have trouble getting it to move at all! They can be lazy and love to keep their humans company. When left alone, basset hounds tend to howl and whine more than the average dog. But who could leave that adorable face?

DOGGIE DATA

Country of Origin:
France

Average Lifespan:
11–12 years

Average Litter Size:
6–8 puppies

Average Weight:
45–75 pounds

Average Height:
11–15 inches

Coat Colors:
7–10 inches

Did You Know?

Basset hounds get their name from the French adjective "bas," meaning "low thing" or "dwarf."

ALL BARK, NO BITE

Beagles are experts at following scents, which makes them useful hunting dogs. They were bred to chase rabbits, so they are small and quick. However, they get distracted easily, so training can be tricky. Beagles are great pets, especially for families with kids, because they have such a calm nature. But be careful—as guard dogs, they tend to befriend strangers instead of warning them away!

Beagles also have a pack mentality, so they like to be around their families and don't like to be left alone. If beagles are left at home for hours at a time, they can develop separation anxiety and very often will howl and bark as a response. They are very chatty dogs and have a different howl for different feelings. Beagles will bark when excited, when they see unfamiliar things, and if they are feeling lonely.

Did You Know?

The Beagle Brigade was created in 1984 as a part of the United States Department of Agriculture's Animal and Plant Health Inspection Service. The Beagle Brigade works at airports, sniffing out disease-carrying pests that may have come in with plants or food.

DOGGIE DATA

Country of Origin:
England

Average Lifespan:
12–15 years

Average Litter Size:
6–10 puppies

Average Weight:
20–25 pounds

Average Height:
13–16 inches

Coat Colors:
Tricolor or white with black and tan or brown and tan

BERNIN' UP

Originally used in Switzerland as working farm dogs that guarded property, Bernese mountain dogs are a large, gentle breed that loves to be outdoors. They have muscular legs that help them navigate rocky, mountainous terrain. The breed is active, but lacks endurance. Bernese mountain dogs are adept at pulling carts due to their sturdy size and friendly personalities and often pull carts in parades or participate in carting competitions.

Bernese mountain dogs are exceedingly patient, which makes them great with children and families. They are loyal dogs but usually attach themselves to one owner and can act aloof with others, though they're still friendly with strangers and other pets. Bernese mountain dogs make great pets, but beware of their shedding! Their fluffy coats need to be brushed often, especially during the spring and fall.

DOGGIE DATA

Country of Origin:
Switzerland

Average Lifespan:
7–8 years

Average Litter Size:
5–7 puppies

Average Weight:
80–120 pounds

Average Height:
23–28 inches

Common Nickname:
Berner

Did You Know?

Many Berner owners have noticed that the breed seems to have a sense of humor, and if its antics make you laugh, it will repeat the action in hopes of getting more laughs!

i ♥ treats

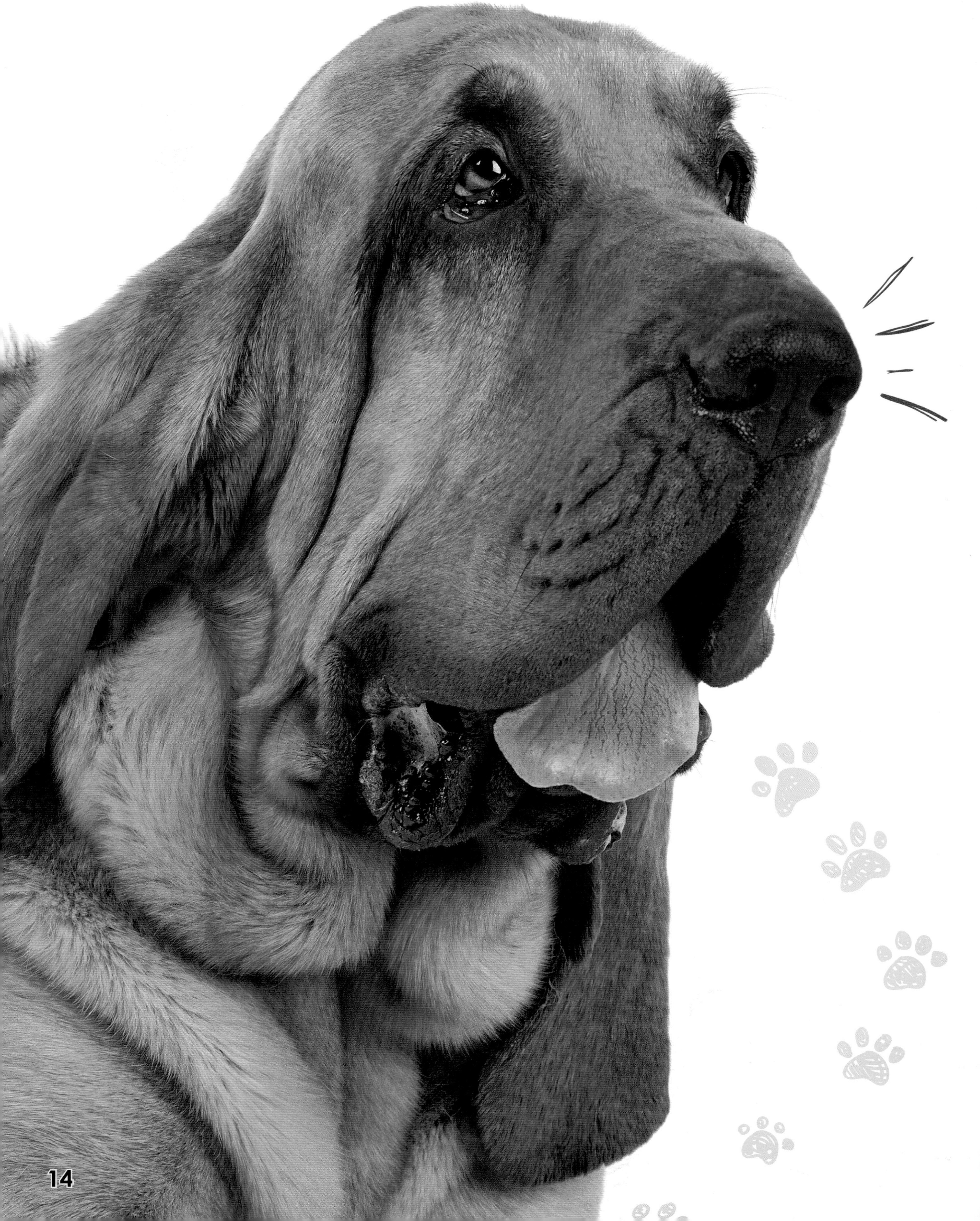

ON THE NOSE

The bloodhound, sometimes called "a nose with a dog attached," was bred to track scents and has an exceptional sense of smell. Bloodhounds can track scents from articles of clothing or other personal belongings and will follow a scent trail for miles. Because of their strong sense of smell, bloodhounds are sometimes used to find missing people. They can follow scents that are hours or even days old because of their sensitive noses.

Gentle and affectionate, the bloodhound makes a great family dog. They are very intelligent, but can be a bit difficult to train due to their single-minded focus—they can be distracted if they find a scent that interests them. Characterized by their long ears and wrinkled faces, bloodhounds are friendly to a fault, so they do not make very good guard dogs. But, not to worry! Someone may be able to make off with your stuff in front of a bloodhound, but the pup can always sniff the items out later!

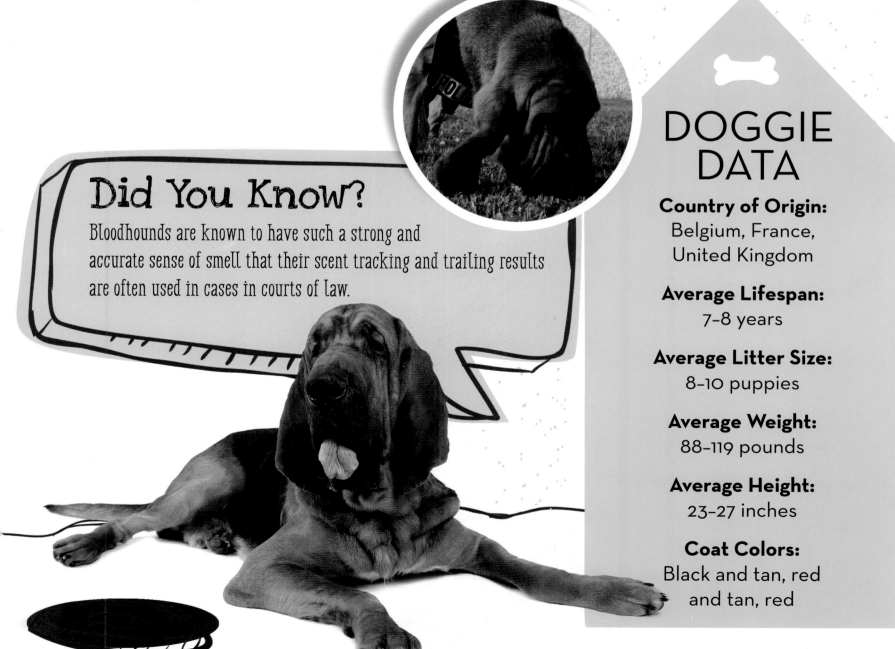

Did You Know?

Bloodhounds are known to have such a strong and accurate sense of smell that their scent tracking and trailing results are often used in cases in courts of law.

DOGGIE DATA

Country of Origin:
Belgium, France, United Kingdom

Average Lifespan:
7–8 years

Average Litter Size:
8–10 puppies

Average Weight:
88–119 pounds

Average Height:
23–27 inches

Coat Colors:
Black and tan, red and tan, red

BLACK TIE PAW-PTIONAL

Boston terriers, characterized by their short statures and square faces, are happy-go-lucky dogs. With their signature black-and-white tuxedo coat, they are always dressed for a paw-ty! Add that to their eager-to-please nature and small size, and these dogs make great pets for families and single owners alike. Although they don't bark very much, they do have flat nostrils that cause them to make snorting and gagging sounds to clear the inside of their noses.

Originally bred to hunt rats, the Boston terrier has since become a beloved companion animal whose only signs of aggression occur when it is protecting its family or owner. Loyal and easy to train, these lovable pups have become increasingly more popular in dog agility competitions, in obedience training, and as therapy dogs. And who could resist a pup who always comes dressed in his best?

Did You Know?

Sergeant Stubby, a Boston terrier, was a decorated war dog in World War I, though they didn't have a name for the breed at the time. He was a hero who comforted the wounded, saved his fellow soldiers from mustard gas attacks, and even captured a German soldier!

DOGGIE DATA

Country of Origin:
The United States of America

Average Lifespan:
13–15 years

Average Litter Size:
1–6 puppies

Average Weight:
10–25 pounds

Average Height:
15–17 inches

Common Nickname:
The American Gentleman

woof

PUT YOUR PAWS UP

DOGGIE DATA

Country of Origin:
Germany

Average Lifespan:
9–15 years

Average Litter Size:
6–8 puppies

Average Weight:
55–71 pounds

Average Height:
21–24 inches

Coat Colors:
Fawn or brindle,
black mask, white markings,
or white

Boxers are sturdy, powerful dogs with formidable jaws that were bred to hold prey for their masters while on the hunt. They are active, athletic dogs and were actually one of the first breeds selected in Germany for police training.

Although their under bite makes them look like they're scowling, boxers are not aggressive dogs. They love human companionship and are happiest when they are spending time with their family. Calm and watchful, they make great guard dogs due to their protective instincts and ability to distinguish between friend and foe. However, don't let this seriousness fool you— boxers take three years to reach maturity, so they stay big puppies for a long time!

Did You Know?

About 18 percent of boxers born white are deaf in one or both ears.

SHORT 'N SNORTY

English bulldogs are easily recognizable by their wide head and shoulders as well as their short, stocky build and enormous under bite. Originally bred for bullbaiting, a cruel practice where bulls were chased and terrorized in order to improve the quality of their meat, English bulldogs used to be ferocious and were known to have a high tolerance for pain. When bullbaiting was outlawed in the 1800s, bulldog lovers preserved the breed as a companion until it became the gentle, friendly dog we know today.

Lazy and sweet, English bulldogs make great family pets and are one of the most popular breeds in America. They tend to slobber and drool a lot, especially after eating or drinking, and they are notorious for loudly snoring and snuffling. Also, because they have such small nostrils, English bulldogs do most of their sweating through their feet!

DOGGIE DATA

Country of Origin:
England

Average Lifespan:
8–10 years

Average Litter Size:
4–6 puppies

Average Weight:
40–50 pounds

Average Height:
14–15 inches

Coat Colors:
Fawn and white, brindle, piebald, red and white

Did You Know?

Yale University's original mascot was an English bulldog named Handsome Dan.

FUNNY FRENCHIE

Bred from a mix of the English bulldog and a terrier, French bulldogs emerged as a smaller companion pet and lap dog. Cheerful and cuddly, a Frenchie's favorite thing to do is be around its family! They love their families so much that they can get separation anxiety if left alone for too long, so a strict regimen of snuggles is recommended for this breed. With their flat noses and faces, small jaws that make them look like they're perpetually smiling, and giant bat-like ears, these pups are pretty huggable!

Nicknames like "clown dog" and "frog dog" have been given to French bulldogs because of their silly personality and the positioning of their hind legs while sitting—similar to a frog's crouch. Frenchies usually have brindle, fawn, or white coats. They are quiet pets, and their size makes them ideal for apartment living, as they don't require much exercise.

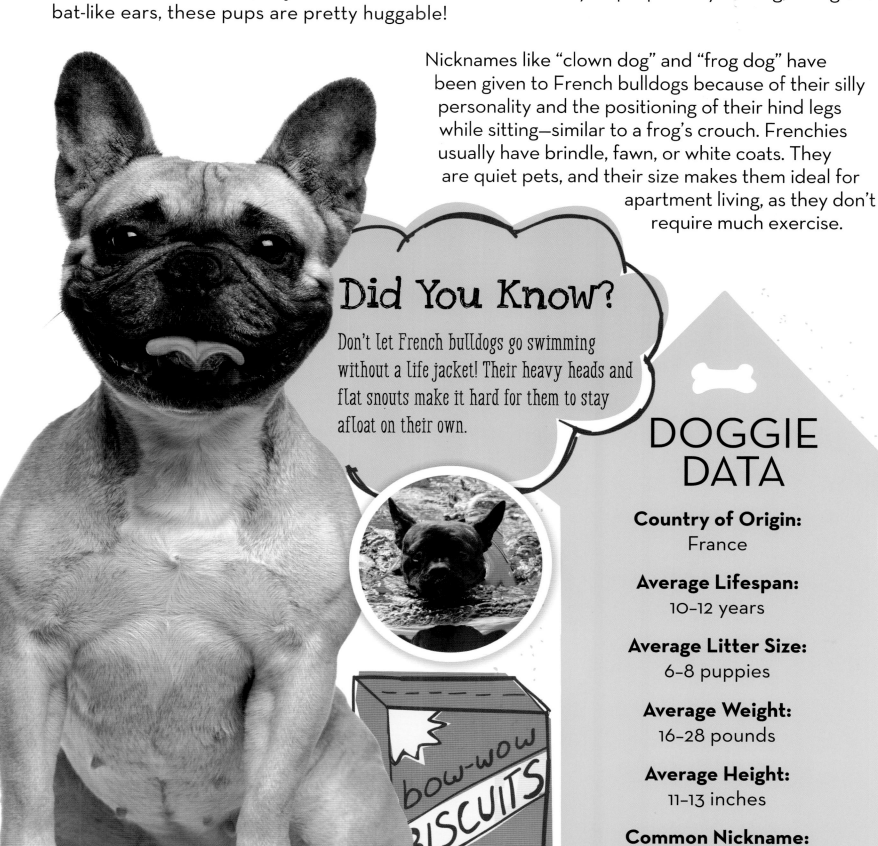

Did You Know?

Don't let French bulldogs go swimming without a life jacket! Their heavy heads and flat snouts make it hard for them to stay afloat on their own.

DOGGIE DATA

Country of Origin:
France

Average Lifespan:
10–12 years

Average Litter Size:
6–8 puppies

Average Weight:
16–28 pounds

Average Height:
11–13 inches

Common Nickname:
Frenchie

PUNY PUPPER

The Chihuahua is the smallest dog breed, weighing in at less than 10 pounds. Named after a state in Mexico, these teeny dogs are perfect companions for owners with small living spaces, as they don't need very much exercise to stay healthy. Chihuahuas can have a long or short coat, and come in a variety of colors (fawn, red, cream, brown, or white).

Chihuahuas are nervous dogs, so they thrive in an environment with patient owners, and do best with adults or older children. They are loyal animals and tend to cling to one person with a fierce love and protective instinct. If you lose a Chihuahua in your house (they are tiny, after all), just check the laundry basket! These pups love to burrow, and can be found snuggling in dark spaces that they view as a den.

DOGGIE DATA

Country of Origin:
Mexico

Average Lifespan:
12–20 years

Average Litter Size:
3–5 puppies

Average Weight:
4–6 pounds

Average Height:
6–9 inches

Common Nickname:
Chi

Did You Know?

Because they were originally desert dogs, Chihuahuas thrive in a warm climate and tend to shiver and tremble when exposed to the cold.

YOU MUST BE LION

Hailing from China, the chow chow is a fluffy, sassy breed also known as Songshi Quan, or "puffy-lion dog." Characterized by its giant cream, red, or brown coat with an especially thick ring of fur around the ruff of its neck, the chow looks like it has a lion's mane. With such a thick coat, chows must be brushed at least four times a week and that should be increased to daily grooming in the fall and spring, when they shed the most.

A beautiful mane is not the only catlike quality a chow possesses. Chows are independent and aloof, friendly to strangers, but only if they are properly introduced by the chow's owner. Chows are intelligent and reserved and need time to get used to new people and environments.

Did You Know?

Chow Chows are the only breed of dog apart from the Chinese Shar-Pei that have blue-black tongues instead of pink ones.

DOGGIE DATA

Country of Origin:
China

Average Lifespan:
11–13 years

Average Litter Size:
3–6 puppies

Average Weight:
45–70 pounds

Average Height:
17–20 inches

Common Nickname:
Chow

HERD is the WORD

Border collies are a common subset of the collie breed. Active and agile, they are frequent winners at athletic competitions and are also hardworking farm dogs. They are widely regarded as one of the most intelligent dog breeds, and it is important to keep them from getting bored, both physically and mentally, or they could become destructive in an attempt to expel extra energy.

Border collies are mostly black and white but can appear in almost every other color variation that is presented in dogs: white, black, tan, red, blue merle, red merle, and more. Their coats are shaggy, but shorter than their Rough collie counterparts, and they have a wider face. Border collies are loyal and easy to train and friendly and ideal for families as long as they are kept active.

Did You Know?

One of the techniques that makes border collies some of the best herders is "the eye." Instead of simply nipping at livestock, border collies get in a crouching position and stare intently at them, intimidating the animals into following the collies' direction.

DOGGIE DATA

Country of Origin:
United Kingdom
(England-Scotland border)

Average Lifespan:
10–17 years

Average Litter Size:
4–8 puppies

Average Weight:
26–44 pounds

Average Height:
19–21 inches

Common Nickname:
Scottish Sheepdog

RUFF AND FLUFF

Collies are a diverse breed with many different subsets. One of the most common subsets of the breed is referred to in the United States as "Rough Collies." Bred for herding sheep in Scotland in the 1800s, the rough collie has a narrow, long face and a beautiful fluffy coat. Typically, rough collies are a sable (or light to medium brown) color with white markings but can be found in black and tan, red and tan, or blue merle.

Rough collies are intelligent, active, and excellent with children. They tend to be shy, so socializing them as puppies with many people and other dogs is key. They are great herders and make useful working dogs. Because their furry coat is so long, they require a lot of grooming, and shed year-round.

Did You Know?

In 1940, Eric Knight published a novel called *Lassie Come Home*, which described the adventures of an intelligent collie named Lassie. The novel was later adapted into a film and television show, which popularized the rough collie to a wide audience.

DOGGIE DATA

Country of Origin:
Scotland

Average Lifespan:
13–15 years

Average Litter Size:
8–12 puppies

Average Weight:
35–75 pounds

Average Height:
21–26 inches

Common Nickname:
Long-Haired Collie

good DoG!

Did You Know?

British Royalty has favored Pembroke Welsh corgis for more than 70 years. Queen Elizabeth II has owned more than 30 during her reign!

SMALL LEGS, BIG DREAMS

The corgi comes in two different, distinct types: the Pembroke Welsh corgi and the Cardigan Welsh corgi. The Cardigan Welsh corgi has a long, fluffy tail, but the Pembroke Welsh corgi is usually born without a tail or has its tail docked at birth, a practice in which the tail is cut off of working breeds to prevent it from getting caught or stuck while they are herding, hunting, or burrowing. Both corgis have the short legs, stocky body, and giant ears that are characteristic of the breed.

Corgis were bred as herding dogs, so they like to herd anything in front of them, even if what's in front of them is their owner on a walk and not a flock of sheep. They are extremely affectionate and loyal, and their intelligence and eagerness to please makes them easy to train. However, this intelligence can backfire when a corgi is feeling mischievous!

DOGGIE DATA

Country of Origin:
Wales

Average Lifespan:
12–14 years

Average Litter Size:
6–8 puppies

Average Weight:
22–31 pounds

Average Height:
10–12 inches

Coat Colors:
Fawn, black and tan, red, or sable, with white markings

SPOT ON

Did You Know?

Dalmatian puppies are born without spots! Spots start appearing 3 to 4 weeks after they are born and grow steadily until they're adults.

DOGGIE DATA

Country of Origin:
United Kingdom

Average Lifespan:
11–13 years

Average Litter Size:
7–8 puppies

Average Weight:
45–70 pounds

Average Height:
19–24 inches

Common Nickname:
Fire House Dog

i ♥ treats

Dalmatians, easily recognizable by their smooth, white coats covered in black spots, have been around since 1791. The breed was ideal for working with the horse-drawn fire engines of the 1800s. The spotted Dalmatians would trot ahead and clear a path so the fire engines could get to an emergency. They are still closely associated with firehouses and are often chosen as the mascot for fire stations.

Dalmatians are very strong, active dogs with impressive stamina. These spotted pups are great companions for runners or hikers and are very loving and protective of their family, but can be aloof around strangers. They are friendly but watchful, making them great guard dogs. Dalmatians are also prone to deafness—about 30 percent of Dalmatians have hearing problems. Though they occasionally have trouble with their hearing, Dalmatians have a keen sense of sight—they don't have issues **spotting** anything!

HOT DOG, HOLD THE BUN

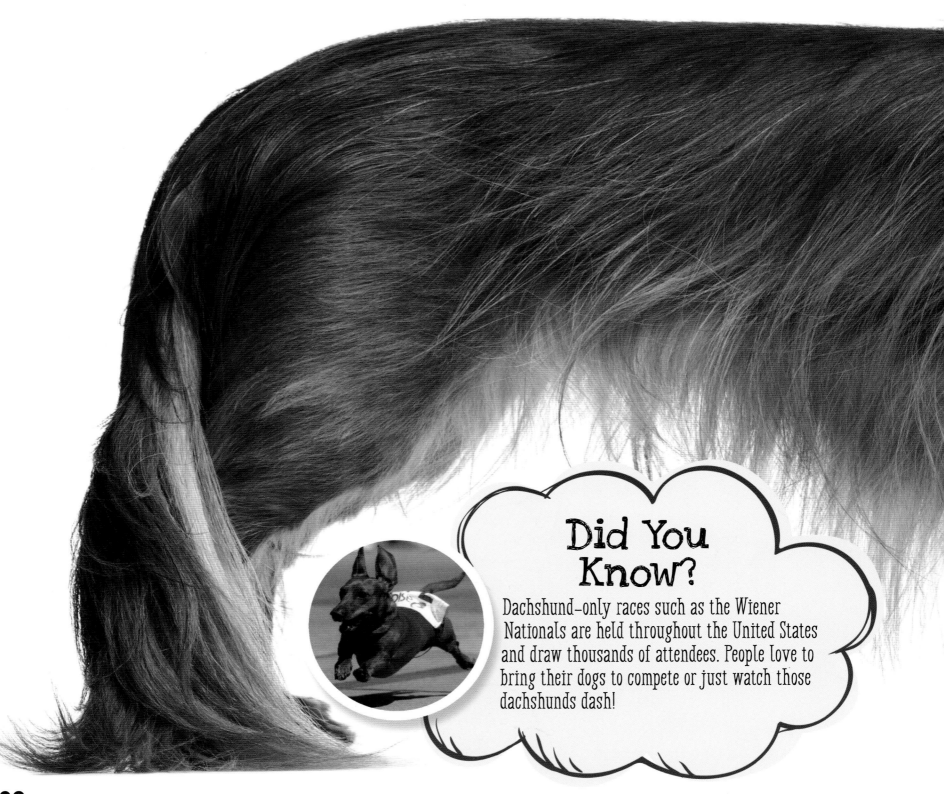

Did You Know?

Dachshund-only races such as the Wiener Nationals are held throughout the United States and draw thousands of attendees. People love to bring their dogs to compete or just watch those dachshunds dash!

The dachshund is characterized by its long body and short legs, a size that was developed to sniff out and chase burrow-dwelling animals like badgers. The dachshund's unusual shape has inspired several nicknames for the breed, such as wiener dog, sausage dog, and hot dog.

A natural-born hunter and burrower, the dachshund can be a stubborn dog to train and is very curious. Dachshunds tend to enjoy burrowing in anything and everything— piles of laundry, dirt in the backyard, or piles of clean laundry after digging in the dirty backyard. However, dachshunds are also known for their devotion and loyalty to their owners.

DOGGIE DATA

Country of Origin:
Germany

Average Lifespan:
12–13 years

Average Litter Size:
4–8 puppies

Average Weight:
16–32 pounds

Average Height:
8–9 inches

Average Length:
12–14 inches

HEROIC HOUNDS

DOGGIE DATA

Country of Origin:
Germany

Average Lifespan:
10–12 years

Average Litter Size:
6–8 puppies

Average Weight:
60–100 pounds

Average Height:
24–28 inches

Common Nickname:
Dobie

Did You Know?

A group of Doberman war dogs helped Americans take back the island of Guam after it was captured by Japanese forces during World War II. A memorial in the likeness of a Doberman war dog stands at the naval base in Guam, honoring the brave Dobermans who died while saving hundreds of human lives. The memorial is called "Always Faithful."

The intimidating figure of the Doberman pinscher is representative of safety and security. Dobermans were bred to be police and war dogs, as they are highly protective and commanding, very athletic, and obedient. Gorgeous dogs with shiny, smooth coats that are typically black with rust-colored markings, Dobermans are very muscular and need a lot of exercise to keep their fit physique!

Dobermans have a fearsome reputation due to their history as guard dogs and police dogs, but in recent years North American Dobermans have been bred to be less aggressive and to become better companion dogs. They love people and are especially protective of their family. With proper socializing in order to be more easygoing around strangers, Dobermans can make great pets!

DOGS ON THE JOB

Developed originally as herding dogs, German shepherds have established reputations as all-purpose working dogs. Identified most commonly as police canines, German shepherds have jobs such as search-and-rescue dogs, bomb-sniffing dogs, therapy dogs, and guide dogs. Because of their intelligence and eagerness to please, German shepherds are a treat to train.

Although they are hard workers, German shepherds also make wonderful family pets. With thick coats in varying colors—most commonly black and sable—and ears that point straight up, German shepherds are beautiful dogs who like to keep busy. They are friendly and obedient, and they pick up on new tasks a lot faster than most breeds. Though they don't give affection as easily as some dogs, they are infinitely loyal to their loved ones.

Did You Know?

In 1928, a female German shepherd named Buddy became the first ever seeing-eye dog. She helped her visually impaired owner, Morris Frank, get around.

USA 15c
Seeing For Me

DOGGIE DATA

Country of Origin:
Germany

Average Lifespan:
7-10 years

Average Litter Size:
7-8 puppies

Average Weight:
50-90 pounds

Average Height:
22-26 inches

Common Nickname:
Deutscher Schäferhund
("German Shepherd Dog"
in German)

GOLDEN RETRIEVERS

Golden retrievers are known for their gentle, sweet, and confident personalities: They love everyone they meet but are especially loyal to their family. They were originally bred to help retrieve waterfowl such as ducks and geese, as well as land birds like grouse and quail, for wealthy Scottish hunters. As a result, goldens are very active and love water sports.

Golden retrievers are double-coated, meaning they have a wavy and water-resistant top coat and a soft, insulating undercoat to keep them warm. True to their name, these pups have golden fur, although the shade can range from a light cream color to a rusty orange. One of the most popular family dogs in the United States, the golden retriever's patience makes it an excellent fit for children. But goldens would rather make friends with strangers than warn them away, so they make very poor guard dogs. They also tend to roam when left to their own devices—on the hunt for even more friends—so make sure to keep a close eye on them!

Did You Know?

Former presidents Gerald Ford and Ronald Reagan both had golden retrievers as pets when they each lived in the White House.

DOGGIE DATA

Country of Origin:
United Kingdom (Scotland)

Average Lifespan:
10–12 years

Average Litter Size:
5–10 puppies

Average Weight:
55–75 pounds

Average Height:
21–24 inches

Coat Colors:
Any shade of gold or cream

GOOD AS GOLD

GENTLE GIANTS

Great Danes are known for their giant size, but their hearts are just as big as they are! Known as "gentle giants," Great Danes were bred to hunt boar, as their massive size and heavy head were useful for holding the boar in place until the hunters could come in for the kill. But, over the years, their tendency to seek out snuggles from their owners has slowly transformed them into companion animals.

Although they are born with floppy ears, breeders used to crop their ears so they wouldn't get caught on anything while hunting, and this practice is continued in some countries. Great Danes also come in a variety of coat colors: fawn with black markings, brindle, black, white with black markings, or blue. They are great with children and make perfect family pets, but make room on the couch! Although they are one of the tallest dogs in the world, these pups don't realize how big they are—as far as they are concerned, they're lap dogs!

Did You Know?

A Great Dane named "Just Nuisance" was the only dog ever to be officially enlisted in the Royal Navy of the United Kingdom. He was a stray that the naval officers fell in love with so they decided to enroll him in the Navy!

DOGGIE DATA

Country of Origin:
Germany

Average Lifespan:
6–8 years

Average Litter Size:
7–10 puppies

Average Weight:
99–200 pounds

Average Height:
28–34 inches

Common Nickname:
Apollo of Dogs

READY, SET, WOOF!

The greyhound has a long, thin, and muscled body with a narrow face and slight frame. Greyhounds were bred to be sighthounds, as their keen eyesight and extremely quick gait were ideal for spotting and hunting small game. Because they are so fast and agile, greyhounds later became racing dogs, participating in racing competitions that still exist today.

Because they are so thin and sleek, greyhounds need soft beds to sleep in so they don't hurt themselves. They enjoy being around their family but are not overly affectionate. Although they are champion racers, they lounge a lot of the time. These pups are better at activities in short bursts than at long-haul hikes and playtime. Smart and quiet, these elegant dogs are winning pets on and off the racetrack.

Did You Know?

Greyhounds have higher levels of red blood cells than other breeds, and lower levels of platelets, so they are often used as universal blood donors by veterinary services.

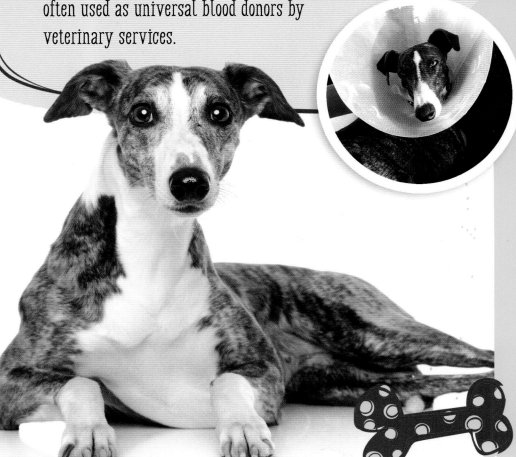

DOGGIE DATA

Country of Origin:
Spain

Average Lifespan:
10–13 years

Average Litter Size:
8–10 puppies

Average Weight:
60–70 pounds

Average Height:
27–30 inches

Common Nickname:
40-mph couch potato

Did You Know?

The Jack Russell terrier can jump up to five times its own height!

BARK!

THE ENERGIZER PUPPY

Fearless, athletic, and with more energy than you would think could fit in such a tiny body: These are the characteristics of the Jack Russell terrier! Originally bred to find foxes in dens, Jack Russell terriers like to keep busy and active. They frequently compete in agility competitions as well as flyball, a relay race done in teams, which involves hurdling and catching a tennis ball.

These tiny dogs have a flurry of energy, and although they can be loving, they make better pets for older children and adults. Despite their size, they're rarely content to be lapdogs and require a lot of exercise to stay stimulated and happy. They can be stubborn, but they're also very intelligent. Their focus is so intense that it's hard not to admire these pups, with their tiny paws and big hearts.

DOGGIE DATA

Country of Origin:
England

Average Lifespan:
12–14 years

Average Litter Size:
5–6 puppies

Average Weight:
9–15 pounds

Average Height:
10–12 inches

WAG YOU'RE IT!

The Labrador retriever is one of the most popular dog breeds in the United States. Characterized by its calm and friendly temperament, the Labrador is often the preferred breed to train as a therapy or service dog. It also has a keen sense of smell and is frequently used as a working dog for police officers, military forces, and hunters.

Labradors come in three distinct coat colors: yellow, chocolate, and black. They are skilled swimmers and have a puppy-like energy beyond their puppy years. Because of their gentle nature, they make great family dogs. However, always keep your eye on your Labrador. They are curious creatures and tend to get interested in something and pursue it endlessly, often leaving at a moment's notice—like when they see a squirrel!

DOGGIE DATA

Country of Origin:
Canada

Average Lifespan:
12–13 years

Average Litter Size:
5–10 puppies

Average Weight:
55–80 pounds

Average Height:
21–24 inches

Coat Colors:
Yellow, dark brown, or black

Did You Know?

Endal the Labrador retriever was a service dog in Britain who became famous for saving a man who had been in an accident. Endal retrieved the man's mobile phone from beneath his car, fetched a blanket and covered him, then ran to a nearby hotel to get help. He was awarded the PSDA's (People's Dispensary for Sick Animals) Gold Medal for Animal Gallantry and Devotion to Duty in 2002.

pdsa
FOR ANIMAL
GALLANTRY
OR DEVOTION
TO DUTY

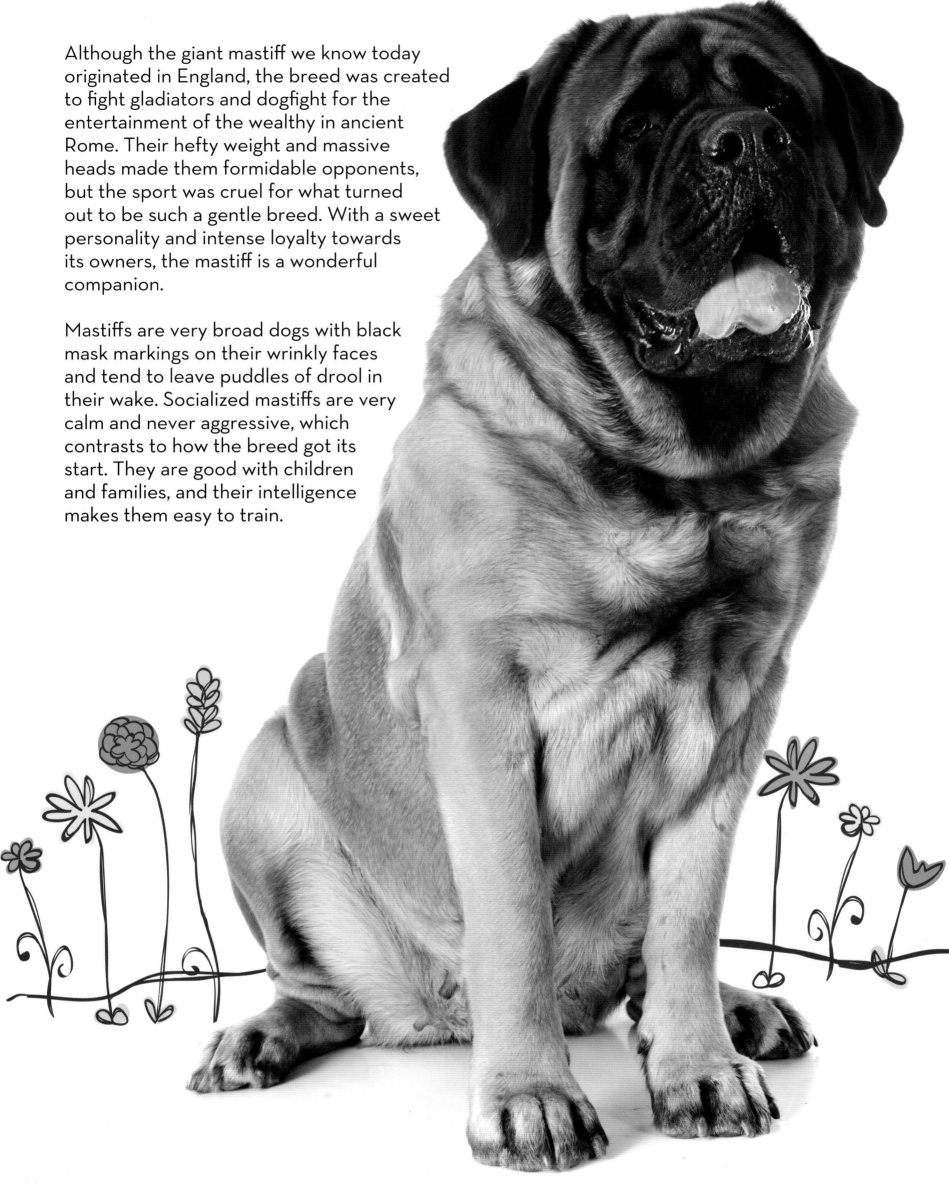

Although the giant mastiff we know today originated in England, the breed was created to fight gladiators and dogfight for the entertainment of the wealthy in ancient Rome. Their hefty weight and massive heads made them formidable opponents, but the sport was cruel for what turned out to be such a gentle breed. With a sweet personality and intense loyalty towards its owners, the mastiff is a wonderful companion.

Mastiffs are very broad dogs with black mask markings on their wrinkly faces and tend to leave puddles of drool in their wake. Socialized mastiffs are very calm and never aggressive, which contrasts to how the breed got its start. They are good with children and families, and their intelligence makes them easy to train.

LARGE
AND IN CHARGE

Did You Know?

The mastiff breed holds the record for the most puppies born in a single litter. In 2004, a mastiff in England gave birth to 24 puppies!

DOGGIE DATA

Country of Origin:
England

Average Lifespan:
6–10 years

Average Litter Size:
10–12 puppies

Average Weight:
120–230 pounds

Average Height:
27–30 inches

Coat Colors:
Fawn, apricot-fawn, silver-fawn, or dark fawn-brindle

DUCK, DUCK, DOG!

Did You Know?

The coat color for black and white Newfies is officially called Landseer, named after Edwin Henry Landseer, an English painter who was beloved for his paintings of animals. He was known for painting dogs in service to humans and painted Newfoundlands often.

DOGGIE DATA

Country of Origin:
Canada

Average Lifespan:
8–10 years

Average Litter Size:
4–12 puppies

Average Weight:
121–176 pounds

Average Height:
26–28 inches

Common Nickname:
Newfies

The cold winds of Canada are no match for the heavy coat of a Newfoundland. The coats of this big breed are waterproof, and they are strong enough to take on rough waves and tides. Newfoundlands are natural swimmers, as they have massive webbed paws, allowing them to propel through the water quickly and efficiently. Newfies also have impressive lung capacities, making them ideal dogs to help with water rescues.

Newfoundlands are known for their giant size, heavy black, brown, or black and white coats, and their mellow personalities. They are known as "nanny dogs" because they are so great with children. Protective and exceedingly gentle, these massive dogs will always look out for their tiny humans. They are devoted guardians and members of the family and have a strong sense of responsibility and duty.

SHAGGY

& WAGGY

The Old English sheepdog is characterized by its gray and white shaggy coat that is so long and fluffy that it often covers its eyes, giving it an endearingly disheveled look. As their name suggests, these fuzzy dogs were bred to help herd sheep and other livestock, so they like having a job to do and may try to herd their family members if no sheep are nearby!

True to their farming origins, Old English sheepdogs do best in wide-open spaces. They have a lot of goofy energy, and their running gait looks more like the ambling of a bear. Fun and fluffy, these dogs are great with families, as they are rarely nervous or aggressive. But their fuzzy coats will need some attention; Old English sheepdogs must be thoroughly brushed at least once a week, a task that could take up to three hours! This is to prevent dirt and debris from mucking up their coats and causing infection or pain. Grooming is a bit of an undertaking, but who could resist those shaggy faces?

Did You Know?

The color, length, and texture of the Old English sheepdog's coat blend in with the sheep it's herding! So, if you spot a sheep licking other sheep, it's probably just an extremely fluffy pup!

DOGGIE DATA

Country of Origin:
England

Average Lifespan:
10–12 years

Average Litter Size:
4–8 puppies

Average Weight:
60–100 pounds

Average Height:
21–22 inches

Coat Colors:
Blue, blue merle, or gray

PRETTY PITTY

The American pit bull terrier, more commonly referred to as a pit or pit bull, is a stocky, short-coated breed with a strong, square head. Pits are closely related to the American Staffordshire terrier, and the two are often mixed up because of their common traits, both physically and temperamentally.

Pit bulls are strong working dogs who are loyal to people. They are protective of their family and very affectionate with their loved ones. These traits make them easy to train, as they are eager to please. Pit bulls' trainability has resulted in their selection as search and rescue dogs and service dogs. Some controversy surrounds these dogs because they were originally bred for dogfighting, and therefore an aggression towards other dogs was encouraged before the cruel practice was outlawed. As such, some countries have banned the breed or placed restrictions owning it. However, as with all dogs, if proper socialization and obedience training are utilized, pits can make loving pets!

DOGGIE DATA

Country of Origin:
The United States of America
The United Kingdom

Average Lifespan:
10–12 years

Average Litter Size:
2–5 puppies

Average Weight:
62–88 pounds

Coat Colors:
black, brindle, fawn,
blue, brown, sable

Did You Know?

Early breeds of pit bulls were known as "nanny dogs" because they were so good with children.

NOT-SO-TALL TAILS

The pint-sized Pomeranian descended from Icelandic sled dogs that were bred to a smaller size in Pomerania, an area near Germany and Poland. This fluffy pup comes in a variety of coat colors like red, white, fawn, sable, black, and tan. Pom poms adore human affection and make great lapdogs. They are quick and active but are always content snuggling with their family.

Although their gorgeous, puffy coats seem high-maintenance, poms are fairly easy to groom, only requiring a short combing a couple of times a week. Pomeranians are inquisitive and confident and will make sure to stay alert to notify their family of any changes to the house. They are happy dogs but can be stubborn when it comes to training, so try your best to stay firm in the face of all that fluff!

DOGGIE DATA

Country of Origin:
Germany/Poland

Average Lifespan:
12–16 years

Average Litter Size:
1–4 puppies

Average Weight:
3–7 pounds

Average Height:
6–7 inches

Common Nicknames:
Pom, Pom Pom

Did You Know?

A group of three or more Pomeranians is called a tuft!

Although poodles are commonly associated with France, their true origins are disputed. Many think they are actually from Germany, because the word "poodle" is similar to the German word "pudel" or "pudelin," meaning "to splash in the water." These pups were bred to be retrievers used in duck hunting and are excellent in the water. Poodles are very intelligent, athletic dogs, so they are often trained for agility and sporting competitions.

Although standard poodles can weigh up to sixty pounds, poodles have been bred in three sizes: standard, miniature, and toy. Their fur is coiled and hypoallergenic, which means it has little likelihood of causing an allergic reaction. Poodles rarely shed, and although their fur is less likely to cause issues for people who are allergic to dog hair, no dog is completely hypoallergenic. Poodles are outgoing and affectionate, but very active, so they need a lot of exercise to stay trim and focused!

Did You Know?

Poodles have a history of their fur being shorn into fancy styles by their owners, but this selective shearing has a purpose besides a fabulous look! For duck hunting, poodles would jump into cold water and needed as little fur as possible slowing them down, but still enough to keep them warm in vital areas.

DOGGIE DATA

Country of Origin:
Germany/France

Average Lifespan:
10–18 years

Average Litter Size:
6–7 puppies

Average Weight:
40–60 pounds

Average Height:
10–15 inches

Coat Colors:
White, brown, gray, brown, black

BIG BRAINS, BIGGER HAIR

PUG AT YOUR HEARTSTRINGS

Pugs are one of the oldest dog breeds and have been the company of royalty throughout history. Characterized by their small size, fawn or black colored coat, short-muzzled face, and curled tail, pugs are known as "a lot of dog in a small space" because of their spunky personalities. Their small muzzle and squished nose makes them snort and snore more than other dogs, but these snuffling pups are hard to resist.

Pugs began as companion dogs and continue to be favorites, as they are fairly easy to train, and their compact size allows them to live in smaller homes. Although pugs are sweet lapdogs with an eagerness to please, it's important that they get regular exercise to prevent obesity. With a strong and sturdy body, pugs are perfect for families with small children because they love to play and are very gentle.

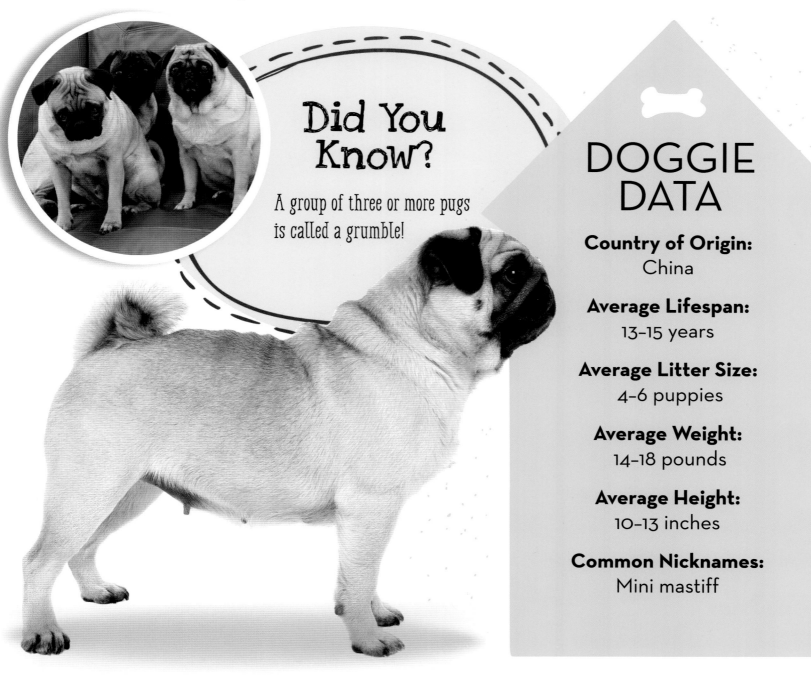

Did You Know?

A group of three or more pugs is called a grumble!

DOGGIE DATA

Country of Origin:
China

Average Lifespan:
13–15 years

Average Litter Size:
4–6 puppies

Average Weight:
14–18 pounds

Average Height:
10–13 inches

Common Nicknames:
Mini mastiff

LAYING DOWN THE PAW

Did You Know?

Rottweilers have a very strong jaw because of their large head. Their bite has a force of 328 pounds, which is about half of the force of a lion's bite!

DOGGIE DATA

Country of Origin:
Germany

Average Lifespan:
8–10 years

Average Litter Size:
8–12 puppies

Average Weight:
77–130 pounds

Average Height:
22–27 inches

Common Nickname:
Rottie

One of the oldest breeds of herding dogs, Rottweilers are thought to have descended from the drover dogs of ancient Rome who aided farmers in bringing livestock to market, but Rotties are most known for pulling carts and herding cattle in Germany. Rottweilers have occasionally been used in movies or television to portray aggressive or vicious guard dogs, which has caused a negative perception of the breed. However, like all dogs with protective instincts, socialization and training show that Rotties can be just as devoted and friendly as other breeds.

Characterized by their large, square head, black and rust-colored coat, and sturdy body, Rottweilers are self-confident, hardworking dogs who enjoy having a job to do. They need quite a bit of exercise to stay stimulated but also enjoy relaxing with their owner. Although they can grow to almost two hundred pounds, Rotties think that they are lap dogs and will snuggle with their humans at every opportunity!

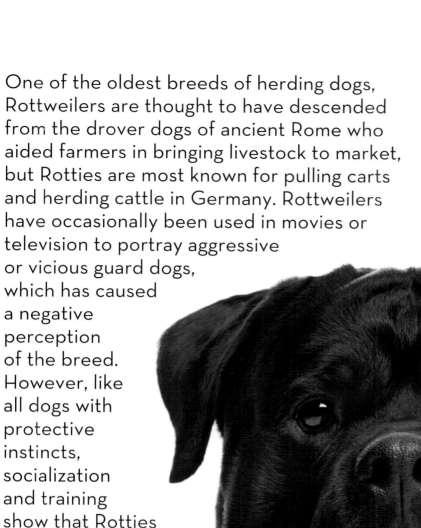

ALL ABOUT

THE SNOUT

Schnauzers come in three distinct breed sizes: giant, standard, and miniature. The standard schnauzer has either a black or salt-and-pepper, wiry coat and long whiskers around its muzzle. The word "schnauzer," translated from German means "snouter," as schnauzers were named for the distinct look of their mustachioed muzzles.

Schnauzers are very smart, energetic, and protective dogs. They were originally bred for hunting rats and guarding the home, so they will alert their owners of intruders with a deep bark.

They require a lot of physical exercise, both for their physical and emotional well-being, and they do well in dog competitions. An active schnauzer is a happy schnauzer! Stubborn but affectionate, these whiskered pups are great for families!

Did You Know?

The mustache-like fur around the standard schnauzer's muzzle has a purpose: it was meant to protect their sensitive face from being scratched or bitten when they hunted rodents!

DOGGIE DATA

Country of Origin:
Germany

Average Lifespan:
13–16 years

Average Litter Size:
4–8 puppies

Average Weight:
30–50 pounds

Average Height:
17–20 inches

Coat Colors:
Salt-and-pepper or black

SHRIEKIN' SHIBA

Did You Know?

Shiba inus are very catlike in their cleanliness. They are known to lick their paws clean, they have dirt-repellant coats, and they often teach themselves not to go to the bathroom in the house.

DOGGIE DATA

Country of Origin:
Japan

Average Lifespan:
12–15 years

Average Litter Size:
1–3 puppies

Average Weight:
15–24 pounds

Average Height:
13–17 inches

Coat Colors:
Red, black and tan,
red with black-tipped hair,
cream, gray, or white

Shiba inus, considered the smallest and oldest of Japan's dog breeds, are very popular companion dogs in Japan. Shibas have thick, double-coated fur, curled tails, and foxlike faces. Bold and independent, Shibas are known for getting along better with cats than with other dogs.

Shiba inus were originally bred as hunters and have a strong prey drive, which can make them spirited when encountering other pups. But these aggressive tendencies can easily be tamed with proper socialization and training. Shiba inus are known for their "shiba scream," a high-pitched noise made when they're excited to see their owner or when they're unhappy with the way they're being petted. Although their scream is distinct, these pups are otherwise very quiet.

NEVER A BAD HAIR DAY

Shih tzus were originally bred as companion dogs and were the pet of choice for Chinese royalty. Also called "chrysanthemum-faced dogs" because of the unusual, flower-like way that their fur grows on their rounded faces, these longhaired pups are friendly and outgoing with people and other dogs alike.

Shih tzus can be stubborn and require training at a young age, but they are also very affectionate and loyal. Although they are alert enough to be watchdogs, they lack the temperament for warning of intruders—they'll usually want to welcome the stranger instead! Shih tzus come in a vast range of coat colors, and their coat is a smooth, silky texture. Their coats are very difficult and expensive to maintain, so some Shih tzu owners cut their hair until they resemble a teddy bear, a style known as the "puppy cut."

DOGGIE DATA

Country of Origin:
China

Average Lifespan:
10–16 years

Average Litter Size:
1–8 puppies

Average Weight:
9–16 pounds

Average Height:
8–11 inches

Common Nickname:
Chrysanthemum Dog

Did You Know?

Underneath the fancy coat of a Shih tzu is the body of an athlete! These fancy pups perform very well in agility competitions, and in 2014 a Shih tzu became the first of its breed to win both a champion title and an agility title.

THERE'S SNOW-BODY FASTER

Did You Know?

In 1925, a team of sled dogs helped deliver medicine to a disease-stricken town called Nome in Alaska. The town was unreachable by any other mode of transportation, so the heroic dogs ran 674 miles in just over 127 hours, and prevented the illness from spreading.

Bred by the Chukchi people of Northeastern Asia as sled dogs, Siberian huskies are built for endurance, speed, and thriving in cold temperatures. They excel in the snow and ice because of their thick coat and are still used in sled racing competitions and to help transport goods in snowy, isolated areas.

Huskies have a variety of coat colors and closely resemble wolves. They have a tendency to howl, rather than bark, and are very vocal. These dogs have also been described as escape artists and need to be contained in a fenced area that is at least six feet high to keep them from escaping. These active dogs need a lot of exercise to stay happy and to prevent boredom, and they love being active with their families. Like wolves, huskies feel a strong connection to their pack, so they need frequent companionship with their family and other dogs.

DOGGIE DATA

Country of Origin:
Siberia/Russia

Average Lifespan:
12-15 years

Average Litter Size:
4-8 puppies

Average Weight:
35-60 pounds

Average Height:
20-24 inches

Common Nickname:
Husky, Sibe

RUFF ROYALTY

The Cavalier King Charles spaniel is based on a spaniel that was a favorite of King Charles II, which is how it got its name. Originally bred for hunting because of their great sense of smell, these spaniels were too small to keep up with long days spent out searching for game and became known as companions rather than working dogs.

Gentle and comforting, Cavies are sweet dogs that get along well with children, adults, and other dogs. These lapdogs are characterized by their round heads, big eyes, and short muzzles. Those big, puppy-dog eyes are difficult to resist when training, but luckily Cavies are very quick learners because they're eager to please. Their long, silky fur requires occasional grooming to keep it from gathering dirt, and they are happy with one walk per day. Low-maintenance, graceful, and incredibly affectionate: these pups make great pets for any family!

Did You Know?

Cavalier King Charles spaniels come in four distinct coat colors, all with special names: Ruby (red), Prince Charles (tri-color), King Charles (black and tan), and Blenheim (chestnut and white).

DOGGIE DATA

Country of Origin:
United Kingdom

Average Lifespan:
12–15 years

Average Litter Size:
2–6 puppies

Average Weight:
13–18 pounds

Average Height:
12–13 inches

Common Nickname:
Cavie

MERRY & HAIRY

Cocker spaniels were originally bred in the United Kingdom, named after the birds they were trained to help hunt: woodcocks. There is a modern English cocker spaniel and an American cocker spaniel; the two are relatively similar, with the American cocker spaniel being smaller. Cocker spaniels have a variety of coat colors but maintain a wavy, shaggy coat and long, curly-haired ears.

Cocker spaniels are very happy and energetic dogs, and although they enjoy physical activity, they are gentle enough to be around small children. They require weekly grooming to maintain the silky quality of their shiny coats, and their long ears are susceptible to bacteria, so they need to be cleaned often. These perky pups are easy to train, but they make terrible guard dogs—they can be too friendly and are more likely to greet an intruder with wagging tails than snarls and barks!

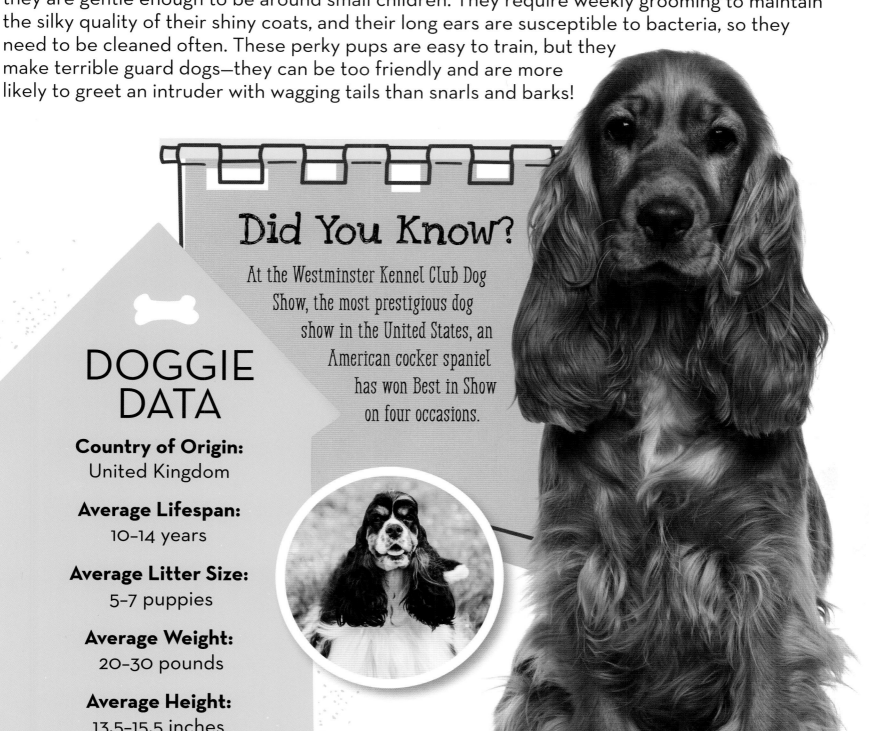

Did You Know?

At the Westminster Kennel Club Dog Show, the most prestigious dog show in the United States, an American cocker spaniel has won Best in Show on four occasions.

DOGGIE DATA

Country of Origin:
United Kingdom

Average Lifespan:
10–14 years

Average Litter Size:
5–7 puppies

Average Weight:
20–30 pounds

Average Height:
13.5–15.5 inches

Common Nickname:
Cockers

SUB-ZERO HERO

Saint Bernards are giant mountain dogs bred for guarding livestock, herding, hunting, and performing search and rescue operations. They would often help find and save people that were caught in avalanches in the Western Alps. These dogs weren't trained but learned search and rescue skills from older dogs. Named for the hospices on the Great and Little St. Bernard Passes in the Western Alps, and located on the borders of Switzerland and Italy and France and Italy, these large dogs were looked after and bred by monks.

Patient and sweet, Saint Bernards are gentle with children apart from accidentally knocking them over with their bulk in excitement over being cuddled. These dogs have big paws, big tails, and most of all big tongues! They are known for drooling more than most dogs, but what's a little saliva between snuggles? With beautiful white and tan coats, thick fur for coping with the cold temperatures, and lovable faces, these huge pups are wonderful family pets!

Did You Know?

Saint Bernard puppies grow very quickly. They are born at only 1.5 pounds and can grow up to 180 pounds. More than one hundred puppy actors were used in the movie "Beethoven's 2nd" because the puppies grew too quickly!

DOGGIE DATA

Country of Origin:
France, Italy, Switzerland

Average Lifespan:
8–10 years

Average Litter Size:
9–10 puppies

Average Weight:
120–180 pounds

Average Height:
26–30 inches

Common Nickname:
Saint

GRAY GHOST

The Weimaraner was bred as a hunting dog to catch large game like deer, boar, and bear in the early nineteenth century. Hard workers with an eagerness to please, these large pups were a favorite of royal hunting parties

Although the shade can vary, Weimaraners are always gray, leading to the nickname "the Gray Ghost." With large eyes and a slender, athletic frame, Weimaraners have a noble look to them. They are very energetic and have impressive stamina, so they require a lot of exercise to stimulate them both physically and mentally. They are loving dogs who devote themselves to their owner and can suffer from extreme separation anxiety when they are left on their own. When Weimaraners are lonely, they bark, whine, and even dig until their owners return, but with proper training and lots of affection, these loyal dogs can be both obedient and calm.

DOGGIE DATA

Country of Origin:
Germany

Average Lifespan:
10–13 years

Average Litter Size:
6–10 puppies

Average Weight:
55–90 pounds

Average Height:
23–27 inches

Common Nickname:
Gray Ghost

Did You Know?

Weimaraners' eyes change color as they age. When they're puppies, they have very light blue eyes, but as they get older they either turn amber or a darker gray-blue color.

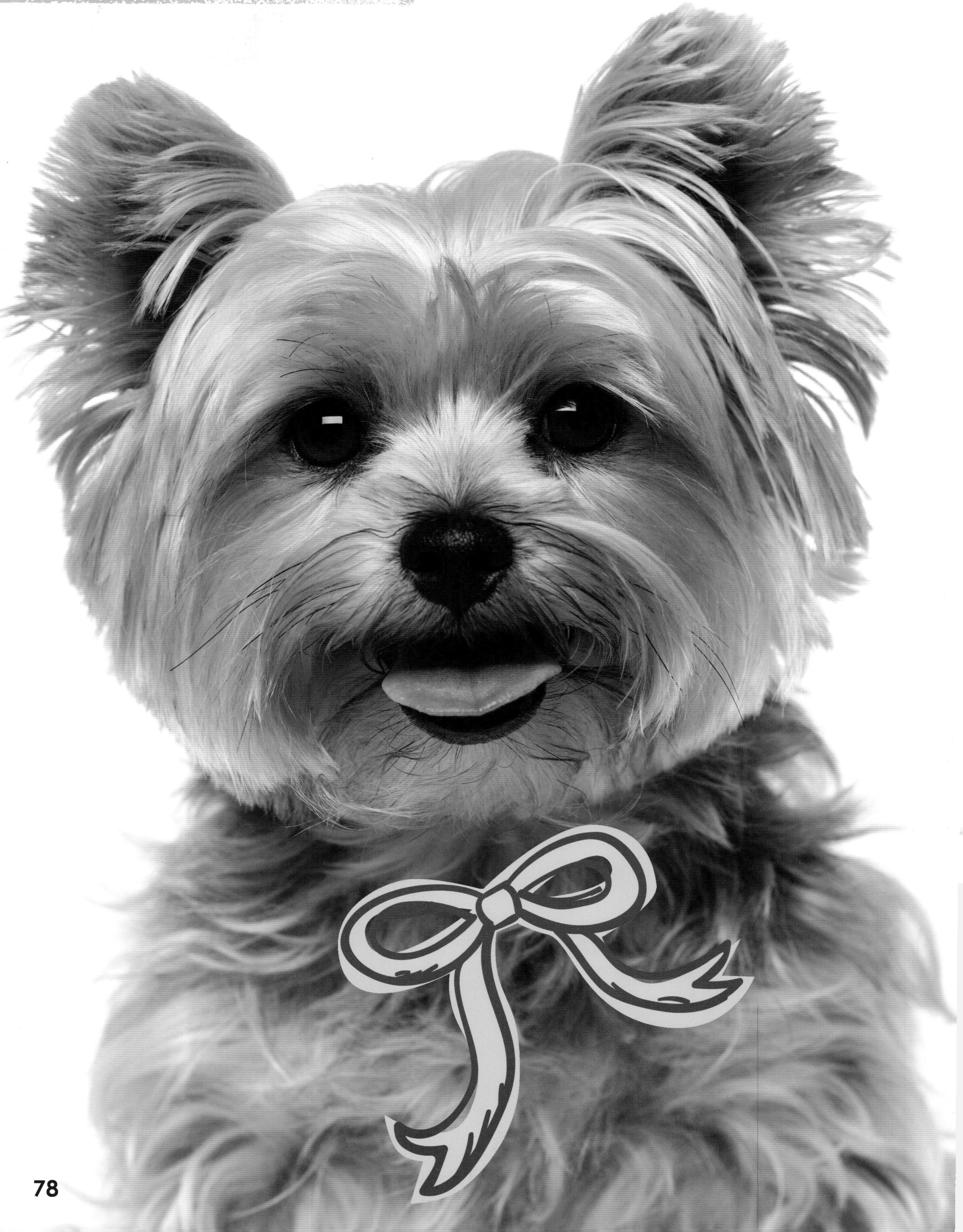

YAPPY AND HAPPY

Yorkshire terriers were bred in England in the nineteenth century to catch rats in clothing mills, but they later became popular as companion dogs. With silky coats that rarely shed, but need daily grooming to keep them from becoming matted or dirty, these pups are fun, family pets. Their coats come in a variety of colors, including black and tan, silver blue and cream, golden, or brown. Because their fur can be a lot to care for, many owners trim their coats to a more manageable length.

These small pups have big personalities! Sassy, curious, and protective, these Yorkies love attention and are better suited for families with older children or adults. Yorkies make great watchdogs and are always on alert for strangers, but this means they bark a lot, and they have quite the yap for such a small dog! Spunky and sweet, Yorkies thrive on love and attention from their owners and make amazing companions.

Did You Know?

If left uncut, a Yorkie's hair can grow up to two feet long!

DOGGIE DATA

Country of Origin:
England

Average Lifespan:
11–15 years

Average Litter Size:
2–5 puppies

Average Weight:
7 pounds

Average Height:
7–8 inches

Common Nickname:
Yorkie

PAWS-ITIVELY PERFECT

Although dogs can vary wildly in size, color, and personality, one thing holds true across the breeds: a dog can be your best friend! With proper care, socialization, training, and love, they will stand by you through thick (treat time) and thin (bath time). Bred for everything from hunting, guarding, and herding to search and rescue, therapy, or companionship, there's nothing a dog can't do. Pick the perfect dog for you and gain a loyal friend for life!